This edition published in the UK in 2020

ISBN- 9798667654162

Text copyright @2020, Mark Evans

No part of this book may be reproduced in any form, or by any means, without prior permission in writing from the author.

MeEducation

Website: **meeducation.net**

Please feel free to contact the author at - **meeducation@yahoo.com**

Also from the same author:

- **Pre Entry English**
- **Entry 1 Reading and Writing**
- **Entry 2 Reading and Writing**
- **Entry 3 Reading and Writing**
- **Level 1 Reading and Writing**
- **level 2 Reading and Writing**
- **Pre Entry Grammar**
- **Entry 1 Grammar**
- **Entry 2 Grammar**
- **Entry 3 Grammar**
- **Level 1 Grammar**
- **Level 2 Grammar**
- **Easy English.**
- **Speaking Grammar**
- **Idioms in English**

 ESOL King

Acknowledgements

The author would like to thank the following colleagues, students, friends and family members for their help and support during the writing and production of this publication:

Dahira Khalid, Eliza Johnson, David and Erika Evans, Alexander Kennedy and Tina Chang.

Mark Evans has been a teacher for over 25 years. He has taught in Australia, Japan, Malaysia and the UK. He graduated in languages from University College London and has a PGCE, CELTA, DELTA, Additional Diploma in ESOL, as well as an MA in English Language Teaching. He currently lives in London where he teaches at a college and a university.

Table of Contents

Unit 1: Food and Catering…………………………… 3

Unit 2: Leisure Activities…………………………. 16

Unit 3: Retail/Hospitality…………………………… 22

Unit 4: Neighbourhood…………………………… 33

Unit 5: Transport…………………………………… 40

Unit 6: Employability……………………………… 49

Unit 7: Health and health care…………………… 59

Unit 8: Money……………………………………… 68

Unit 9: Maths……………………………………….. 74

Unit 10: Citizenship………………………………… 78

Unit 11: Countries/Festivals………………………… 83

Unit 12: Describing – people, family…………… 91

Unit 1: Food and Drink – Vocab

Put the food and drink in the right list:

banana	potato	carrot	beer	onion
lamb	broccoli	pie	orange	pork
chicken	apple	wine	strawberry	milk
bread	coffee	peas	spaghetti	tea
pizza	rice	bacon	pear	beef

Fruit	Vegetables	Meat	Drink	Other

Extension - Think of more to add to the list:

Food and Drink

Breakfast	food you eat at midday
Lunch	you want to drink something
Dinner	not sweet
Spicy	very nice to eat
Delicious	you can't eat any more
Full	food you eat in the morning
Starving	no taste
Bland	food you usually eat at night
Sour	very hungry
Thirsty	Hot

1) favourite/food/what/is/your?

2) drink/what/your/is/favourite?

3) like/you/do/food/spicy?

4) for/eat/what/do/breakfast/you?

5) eat/what/you/do/lunch/for?

6) usually/eat/you/do/for/dinner/what?

7) favourite/snack/what/your/is/country/your/in?

8) like/you/food/British/do?

9) what/drink/you/do/when/thirsty/are/you?

10) you/do/like/sweet/sour/or/food?

11) cook/good/you/are/a?

12) many/tea/or/how/a/of/in/cups/coffee/you/day/do/drink?

Extension – Write at least 5 more questions to ask your partner:

Catering – people in a restaurant

> He shows you to your seat( )   She gives you the bill( )
> He makes coffee( )   He cooks food( )   He pays the wages( )
> He is in charge( )   He mops the floor( )   He dries the dishes( )
> He serves coffee( )   He gives you the menu( )
> She takes your order( )   He gives food to the waiter( )
> He cleans the restaurant( )   He puts dishes in the dishwasher( )

Match what people do to the job:

1) Waiter: _____

_____

2) Waitress: _____

_____

3) Barista: _____

_____

4) Cook/chef: _____

_____

5) Manager: _____

_____

6) Cleaner: _____

_____

7) Kitchen porter: _____

_____

Wallace the Waiter

Wallace works in an Italian restaurant in London. He is a waiter and he works five days a week.

He starts work at 5pm. He puts on his uniform. First, he cleans the tables and mops the floor. Later, he puts the cutlery on the table.

At 6pm he opens the restaurant. He welcomes the customers and takes them to their table. He gives them the menu. Next, he takes their order. Then, he goes to the kitchen to tell the chef. The chef cooks the food and gives it to Wallace. He takes it to the customer.

When the customers have finished he gives them the bill. He takes the money and gives them the change.

The restaurant closes at 11pm. Then he tidies up and goes home at 12am.

1) What is Wallace's job?

2) Where does he work?

3) What time does he start?

4) What job does he do first before the restaurant opens?

5) What does he do at 6pm?

6) What time does the restaurant close?

7) What does he do after the restaurant closes?

8) What time does he finish work?

Extension – Write at least 3 more questions about the text:

Tools of a Kitchen Porter

knife	spoon	fork	dish
sponge	washing up liquid	glass
tea towel	sink	dishwasher

1) _____

2) _____

3) _____

4) _____

5) _____

6) _____

7) _____

8) _____

9) _____

10) _____

Now put the words in alphabetical order:

1 _____ 2 _____ 3 _____ 4 _____ 5 _____

6 _____ 7 _____ 8 _____ 9 _____ 10 _____

Kevin the Kitchen Porter

Kevin is a kitchen porter in a busy restaurant. The restaurant is in Harrow in London. Ten people work in the restaurant.

He starts at 6pm. The waiter gives Kevin the dirty dishes, knives, forks and spoons. He also gives him cups and glasses. Kevin puts them in the dishwasher and presses the button.

He waits 5 minutes and then he opens the dishwasher. He takes the clean dishes, knives, forks and spoons out of the dishwasher. He also takes the cups and glasses out carefully. Then he puts them away.

He finishes work at 12am. Then he goes home by bus. He likes his job but it is very hard.

1) What is Kevin's job?

2) Where is the restaurant?

3) Is the restaurant busy?

4) What time does he start?

5) How long does he wait for the dishwasher?

6) What time does he finish?

7) How does he go home?

8) Does he like his job?

Extension – Write at least 3 more questions about the text:

Food Hygiene - Vocab

Kitchen paper	Plunger	Chopping board
Hand wash	Tap	Sink	Bin
Hair net	Gloves	Overalls/apron

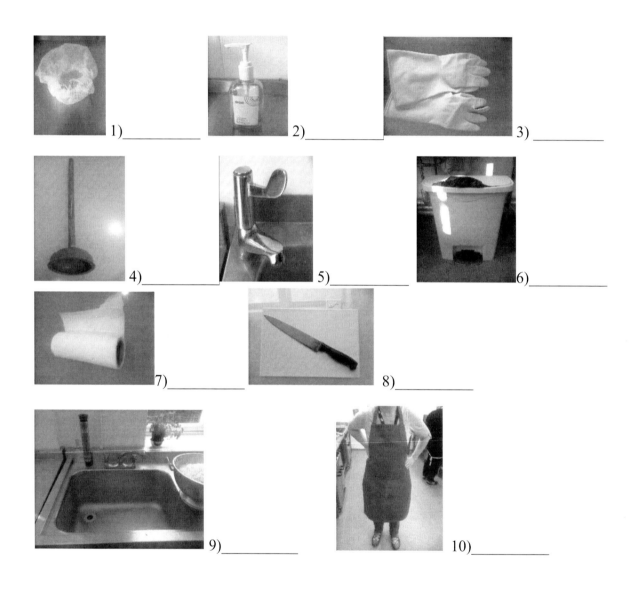

1) _____
2) _____
3) _____
4) _____
5) _____
6) _____
7) _____
8) _____
9) _____
10) _____

Now put the words in alphabetical order:

1_____ 2_____ 3_____ 4_____ 5_____

6_____ 7_____ 8_____ 9_____ 10_____

Chopping Boards

Match the board colours with the types of food:

Green   dairy/bread

Red   fish

White   cooked meat

Blue   raw meat

Yellow   vegetables

---

cheese   salmon   cucumber   butter   minced meat
onion   cooked bacon   lettuce   bread   ham   cod
tomato   raw steak   tuna   raw bacon   salami
cooked steak   raw lamb   haddock   bun

Which foods do you cut on which coloured boards?

Green	Red	White	Blue	Yellow

(If you finish early, add some more)

Job Advertisement

> **Wanted Urgently: Chef**
>
> Chef needed for busy Italian restaurant in west London. Immediate start.
>
> Hours: 5pm – 11pm. Mon – Fri. Hourly rate: £7. 10 days' holiday. Perks: free meals and free uniform.

Read the job advert and answer the questions:

1) What is the job?

2) What kind of restaurant is it?

3) Where is the job?

4) When does the job begin?

5) What time does the job start?

6) What time does the job finish?

7) What are the wages?

8) What are the perks?

Cleaning - Vocab

mop   bucket   cloth   dust   dustpan   brush   stain   detergent   broom

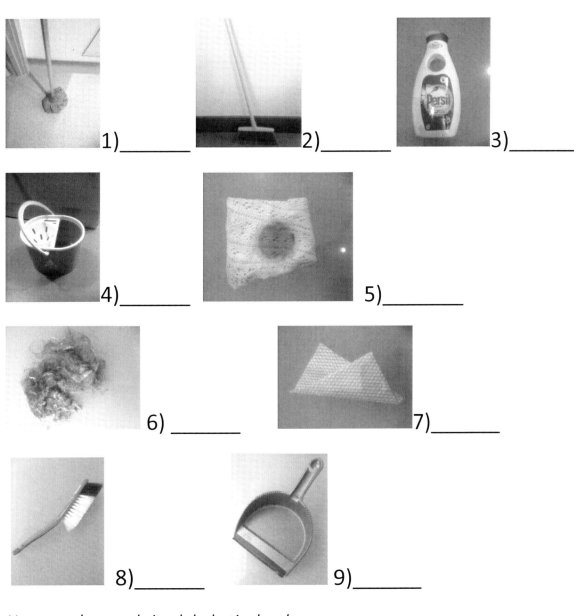

1)_____ 2)_____ 3)_____

4)_____ 5)_____

6)_____ 7)_____

8)_____ 9)_____

Now put the words in alphabetical order:

1_____ 2_____ 3_____ 4_____ 5_____

6_____ 7_____ 8_____ 9_____

Colin the Cleaner

Colin is a cleaner. He cleans in an office in central London.

He starts at 5am. First, he mops the floor in the kitchen with water and a bucket. Next, he vacuums the floor. He vacuums 5 floors. Then he cleans the windows. He dusts all the desks in the office with a clean cloth. He cleans the toilets on every floor. He is proud of his work.

He finishes at 9am and takes the bus home. The bus takes one hour. He likes his job but it is very hard work.

1) Where does Colin work?

2) What time does he start?

3) Where does he mop?

4) What does he vacuum?

5) How many floors does he vacuum?

6) What does he dust?

7) What time does he finish?

8) Does he like his job?

Extension – Write at least 3 more questions about the text:

Cleaning Questions

1) you/like/do/cleaning?

2) your/is/very/home/clean?

3) did/you/home/when/your/clean/last?

4) you/home/clean/how/do/often/your?

5) clean/your/do/you/windows?

6) have/you/a/cleaner/vacuum/do?

7) do/buy/where/your/products/cleaning/you?

8) a/do/have/you/dishwasher?

9) clothes/often/do/how/wash/you/your?

10) washing/use/what/do/powder/you?

11) bath/do/take/you/shower/a/or?

12) often/how/bath/you/do/take/a?

13) how/do/bathrooms/many/have/you?

14) your/clean/is/neighbourhood?

Extension – make at least 3 more questions to ask your partner:

Job Advertisement

> **Wanted Urgently: Cleaner**
>
> Cleaner required for busy 200-bed hotel in central London. Immediate start.
>
> Hours: 8am – 4pm. Mon – Fri. £8 per hour. 20 days' holiday. Perks: free meals and free uniform.

Read the job advert and answer the questions:

1) What is the job?

2) How many rooms does the hotel have?

3) Where is the job?

4) When does the job begin?

5) What time does the job start?

6) What time does the job finish?

7) What are the wages?

8) What are the perks?

Unit 2: Leisure Activities

Match the words to the meanings:

	Kicking a ball
	Moving your body to music
	Throwing a ball into a net
	Riding a bicycle
	Moving black and white pieces on a board
	Making food
	Going to many places
	Moving your body in water
	Buying things in shops
	Riding a horse

basketball   cooking   chess

cycling   dancing   football   horse riding

shopping   swimming   travelling

Extension - now put the words in alphabetical order:

1_____ 2_____ 3_____ 4_____

5_____ 6_____ 7_____ 8_____

9_____ 10_____

Leisure Questions

Put these in order to make questions:

1) like/you/football/do?

2) sports/what/you/like/do?

3) did/sports/do/you/country/your/in?

4) have/do/you/bike/a/?

5) dancer/are/good/a/you?

6) play/can/you/chess?

7) you/like/do/shopping?

8) your/what/favourite/shop/is?

9) like/you/do/travelling?

10) you/are/cook/a/good?

11) cook/what/did/yesterday/you?

12) do/what/you/do/at/weekend/the?

Extension - Write at least 3 more questions about this topic to ask your partner:

David's Favourite Activities

David likes many sports. On Monday he plays football. He is in the football club. He plays after school for 2 hours. On Tuesday he plays chess. After school he studies French. He doesn't like French. On Wednesday he plays computer games after school. His favourite hobby is playing computer games. He plays for 2 hours. On Thursday he studies maths after school for 45 minutes. He doesn't like maths. On Friday he watches TV after school.

On Saturday he does judo. On Sunday he is free. He relaxes. He goes to church at 10am. Sunday is his favourite day.

1) What day does he play football?

2) What day does he play chess?

3) Does he like studying French?

4) What is his favourite hobby?

5) What does he do on Friday?

6) When does he do judo?

7) When is he free?

8) What is his favourite day?

Extension – Write at least 3 more questions about the text:

Daily Routines - David's Day

David wakes up at 6:45am. He stretches and then gets out of bed at 7 o'clock. He goes downstairs and eats breakfast. He has egg on toast and a glass of orange juice. He takes a shower at 7:30 and brushes his teeth. Then he gets dressed. He leaves his house at 7:45 and walks to school. He gets to school at 8:30. He studies at school for 3 hours. He has lunch at 12:30. He leaves school at 4:30. He gets home at 5. At 6 he eats dinner. After dinner he watches TV. He goes to bed at 10 and reads a book in bed. He sleeps at 10:30.

1) What time does David wake up?

2) What does he eat for breakfast?

3) When does he leave his house?

4) How does he get to school?

5) What time does he eat lunch?

6) What time does he get home?

7) What does he do after dinner?

8) When does he go to bed?

9) What does he do in bed?

10) What time does he sleep?

Extension – write at least 3 more questions about the text:

What do you do every day?

eat lunch   wake up   EAT DINNER   sleep

study   go home   go to college   watch TV

brush teeth   have breakfast   have a break

get dressed   go to bed   get undressed

have a shower   get home

Put the verbs into the boxes:

Morning (6am-12pm)	Daytime (12pm – 5pm)	Evening/Night (5pm – 6am)

Extension – add more verbs to the boxes above

Daily Routine Questions

1) do/time/what/get/up/you?

2) you/take/shower/bath/or/do/a?

3) often/how/brush/teeth/you/your/do?

4) usually/eat/what/do/breakfast/you/for?

5) drink/for/what/you/do/breakfast?

6) leave/house/your/time/what/do/you?

7) usually/eat/what/lunch/you/for/do?

8) drink/lunch/for/what/you/do?

9) do/eat/you/where/lunch?

10) eat/who/with/do/you/lunch?

11) time/home/go/you/do/what?

12) go/how/do/home/you?

13) home/get/time/what/you/do?

14) usually/what/eat/do/dinner/you/for?

15) you/after/what/do/dinner/do?

16) or/morning/wash/you/the/night/do/in/at?

17) what/time/usually/you/bed/go/do/to?

18) sleep/what/time/you/do?

Extension – write at least 3 more questions to ask your partner:

Unit 3: Retail - vocab

bag	change	basket
till	shop	wallet	trolley
purse	receipt	aisle

 1)_____  2)_____  3)_____

 4)_____ 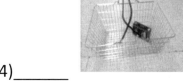 5)_____  6)_____

 7)_____  8_____

 9)_____  10)_____

Now put the words in alphabetical order:

1_____ 2_____ 3_____ 4_____ 5_____

6_____ 7_____ 8_____ 9_____ 10_____

Shopping

Till   low price
Expensive   place where you pay
Greengrocer   paper you get from a shop
Receipt   fruit and vegetable shop
Cheap   high price
Sale   the person you pay in a shop
Cashier   everything is a low price

1) like/you/shopping/do?

2) where/you/do/shopping/usually/go?

3) your/shop/favourite/what/is?

4) in/London/what/is/shop/the/biggest?

5) in/your/what/biggest/the/shop/is/country?

6) you/do/where/your/clothes/buy?

7) who/you/usually/do/shop/with?

8) buy/what/did/last/week/you?

9) what/you/are/going/to/next/week/buy?

10) buy/where/your/you/food/do?

11) every/much/you/how/do/spend/week?

12) often/go/how/shopping/you/do?

Extension – write at least 5 more questions to ask your partner:

Simon's Supermarket

Simon's supermarket opens at 7am and closes at 10pm. It is a big supermarket in Richmond and 20 people work there.

It sells fruit and vegetables, meat and even clothes. Every January they have a sale and you can get many bargains.

You can pick up a basket and walk around and choose the things you want to buy. You put things in the basket. Then you go to the till to pay. You give the cashier your money. The cashier gives you a receipt and you put things into a bag and go home.

1) What time does Simon's supermarket open?

2) What time does it close?

3) Where is Simon's supermarket?

4) How many people work there?

5) What does it sell?

6) When is the sale?

7) Where do you pay?

8) What does the cashier give you?

Extension – write at least 3 more questions about the text:

Sally's Shopping Trip

Yesterday Sally _____ (go) on a shopping trip with her friend Mary. She _____ (wake) up at 9am and _____ (get) dressed. She _____ (walk) to the bus stop and _____ (wait) for the bus. She _____ (take) the bus to Oxford Street. She _____ (meet) Mary at 11 o'clock and they both _____ (go) shopping. First they _____ (go) to Selfridges and _____ (look) at many clothes. Sally _____ (buy) a red dress. It _____ (cost) £80. She _____ (pay) at the till and _____ (take) her change.

At 1 o'clock they _____ (have) lunch in a restaurant. Sally _____ (eat) pasta and Mary _____ (eat) a panini. They both _____ (drink) a small glass of wine. The food _____ (be) delicious. After they _____ (drink) a cup of coffee. The bill _____ (be) £20. They _____ (pay) the waiter and _____ (leave) the restaurant.

After lunch they _____ (go) to another shop. They both _____ (buy) a pair of shoes. They _____ (pay) by credit card. They _____ (say) goodbye to each other and they _____ (take) the bus home.

Sally _____ (arrive) home at 8 o'clock. She _____ (drink) a cup of tea. She _____ (be) very tired and _____ (have) a bath. Then she _____ (go) to bed. She _____ (sleep) straight away.

Questions

1) When did Sally go on a shopping trip?

2) Who did she go with?

3) What time did she wake up?

4) Where did she take the bus to?

5) What colour was the dress?

6) How much was the dress?

7) What time did they eat lunch?

8) What did they eat in the restaurant?

9) How much was the bill?

10) What time did Sally arrive home?

11) What did Sally drink at home?

12) What did she do after her bath?

Extension – write at least 3 more questions about the text:

Job Advertisement

> **Wanted: Shop Assistant**
>
> Shop Assistant required for busy supermarket (Asda) in Camden. Start: Friday.
>
> Hours: 9am – 5pm. Mon – Sat. £7 per hour. 25 days' holiday. Perks: staff bonus and free uniform.

Read the job advert and answer the questions:

1) What is the job?

2) What is the name of the supermarket?

3) Where is the job?

4) When does the job begin?

5) What time does the job start?

6) What time does the finish?

7) What are the wages?

8) What are the perks?

Hospitality - Vocab

Reception	Lobby	Receptionist
Duvet	Double room	Luggage	Pillow
Sheet	Bar	Mattress

 1)_____   2)_____  3)_____

 4)_____  5)_____

 6)_____  7)_____  8)_____

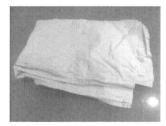 9)_____  10)_____

Now put the words in alphabetical order:

1_____ 2_____ 3_____ 4_____ 5_____

6_____ 7_____ 8_____ 9_____ 10_____

Rodger the Receptionist

Rodger is a receptionist in a busy hotel in central London. The hotel has 200 rooms.

He starts his shift at 5am. He greets the guests at reception. First, he takes the names of the guests and inputs them into the computer. Next, he gives them a room: a single room or a double room. Then he gives them the key. The guests take their luggage to their room.

Rodger finishes his shift at 10pm. It is a long day but he enjoys his job. He takes the bus home and relaxes with his family.

Answer the questions about the text:

1) Where does he work?

2) Is the hotel busy?

3) How many rooms does the hotel have?

4) What time does he start his shift?

5) Who does he greet at reception?

6) What do the guests take to their room?

7) What time does he finish his shift?

8) Does he enjoy his job?

Extension – make at least 3 more questions about the text:

Conversation at a hotel reception

Who says what? First read the text. Then put "R" for the receptionist and "G" for the guest. Next put the sentences in the right order.

___A) Yes, please. Can I have a room? ___

___B) 4 nights, please. ___

___C) Double, please. ___

___D) Here you are. ___

___E) Single or double? ___

___F) How many nights? ___

___G) OK, sir. That is £400. ___

___H) Thank you! Have a nice stay! ___

___I) Can I help you, sir? ___

___J) Thank you! Goodbye! ___

Now practise with your partner:

Hotels – Vocab and Questions

Match the words with their definition:

Check in	Sheets, blankets, pillowcases
Check out	Bags
Luggage	Go to reception to give back keys
Linen	Go to reception to get keys
Rate	Available room
Vacancy	Someone who cleans the rooms
Chambermaid	Staff that parks the guests' cars
Valet	Cost of room

1) did/a/when/stay/you/hotel/last/in?

2) you/do/hotels/like?

3) your/what/favourite/is/hotel?

4) is/your/what/best/in/the/hotel/country?

5) hotel/what/the/in/is/country/biggest/your?

6) a/is/hotel/how/country/much/your/in?

7) many/hotels/are/you/there/live/where?

8) to/work/would/you/in/like/hotel/a?

Extension – make at least 3 more questions to ask your partner:

Job Advertisement

Wanted: Receptionist

Receptionist needed for busy 400-bed hotel in west London. Start next month.

Hours: 7am – 5pm. Hourly rate: £7. 50 days' paid holiday. Perks: free meals and free uniform.

Read the job advert and answer the questions:

1) What is the job?

2) How many rooms does the hotel have?

3) Where is the job?

4) When does the job begin?

5) What time does the job start?

6) What time does the job finish?

7) What are the wages?

8) What are the perks?

Unit 4: Neighbourhood - Vocab

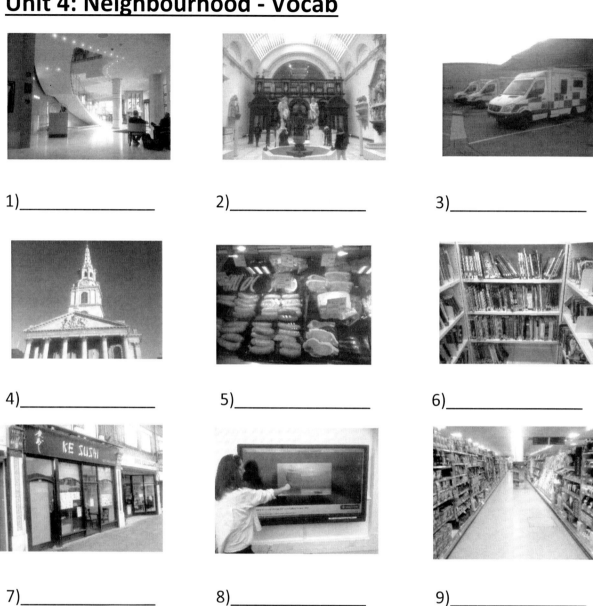

1)_____ 2)_____ 3)_____

4)_____ 5)_____ 6)_____

7)_____ 8)_____ 9)_____

Match the places to the pictures:

school   butcher shop   library   church   museum

hospital   hotel   supermarket   restaurant

Now sort them into alphabetical order:

1)_____ 2) _____ 3)_____ 4)_____ 5)_____

6)_____ 7)_____ 8)_____ 9)_____

Billy's Town

Billy lives in Barnes. Barnes is a nice suburb near the river Thames. It is a wealthy area; people have a lot of money. He lives in a big house with four bedrooms and two bathrooms. He has a big garden with a lawn and many flowers.

In Barnes there are two supermarkets, a butcher shop, a post office and three barbers. There are three charity shops. There are also many restaurants: Indian, French, Italian and Chinese. There is a big park with swings and slides. He plays there with his friends.

There are three schools. All the schools are very good. Billy's school is eight minutes' walk from his house. He loves his school.

1) Where does Billy live?

2) Where is Barnes?

3) How many bedrooms does his house have?

4) How many supermarkets are there?

5) How many charity shops are there?

6) What does the park have?

7) How far is Billy's school?

8) Does Billy like his school?

Extension - make at least 3 more questions to ask your partner:

David's Neighbourhood – Literacy Check

david live in richmond richmond is a very nice Place in south-west london. It is a very old town with many nice old building. Their is big station with trains to london. Their is many old church in town which are more than a hundred year old. Their is big libery where you can reed books.

There are many shop in richmond. There are thre suparmarket, to bakerys and many cloths shop. If you want to drink coffe, there is many cafe.

At night there is a lot to do. There is about twelf pub where you can drinking beer. There is also money restarants - italian, french, german and chinese. David lick italian fod bestest.

David lick his neigberhod.

Correct the mistakes and write in the box below:

Questions:

1) Where does David live?

2) Where is Richmond?

3) Where do the trains go to?

4) How old are the churches?

5) How many supermarkets are there?

6) How many bakeries are there?

7) How many pubs are there?

8) What food does David like best?

Now write about your neighbourhood:

Neighbourhood

Match the places to things you can do there:

Post office	have a haircut
Shoe shop	eat food
Barber	wash your clothes
Restaurant	look for work
Laundrette	buy a newspaper
Hospital	buy some shoes
Newsagent	drink beer
Job centre	buy some stamps
Pub	visit a doctor

1) where/you/do/live?

2) address/what/your/is?

3) you/like/do/your/town?

4) many/supermarkets/there/are/how?

5) where/your/is/centre/job?

6) you/like/do/restaurants?

7) restaurant/what/your/is/favourite?

8) your/favourite/what/is/supermarket?

9) like/you/do/pubs?

10) you/where/your/do/clothes/buy?

11) haircut/have/where/do/a/you?

12) you/go/to/do/library/your?

Extension – Make at least 3 more questions about neighbourhood:

Kevin's Coffee Shop

Kevin works in a coffee shop in Glasgow. He works there six days a week. Every day he leaves his house at 6am and he arrives at work at 6:30.

First he turns on the equipment and takes deliveries. He opens the coffee shop at 7am. He takes the orders from the customers and then takes payment. His break is at 11am for one hour.

After his break he goes back to the coffee shop. He serves customers all day. At 5pm he closes the shop. He tidies up the tables and then he sweeps the floor. He goes home at 6pm.

1) Where does Kevin work?

2) How often does he work?

3) What time does he start?

4) What does he do first?

5) What time does he open the coffee shop?

6) What time is his break?

7) What time does he close the coffee shop?

8) What does he do after the coffee shop closes?

Extension – make at least 3 more questions about the text:

Neighbourhood

Across
3. you learn here
5. you can buy a pint of beer here
8. you can buy beef and pork here
9. you can send a parcel from here
10. you can play here
13. when you are very sick you go here
14. you can watch a film here
16. you can get money from here
17. you can buy medicine here
18. you park your car here
19. you go here if you need the police

Down
1. you can buy a dog here
2. you can take a train from here
4. you can take a bus from here
6. you can buy washing powder here
7. when you are sick you visit here
11. you pray here in the UK
12. you can rent a flat/house from here
15. you can borrow books from here

Unit 5: Transport – Names of Transportation

1)_____ 2_____ 3)_____

4)_____ 5)_____ 6)_____

7)_____ 8)_____ 9)_____ 10)_____

Extension – cover the words below and see if you can spell them:

train	van	motorbike	
bike	bus	lorry	moped
boat	plane	tram	

Now put the words in alphabetical order:

1_____ 2_____ 3_____ 4_____ 5_____
6_____ 7_____ 8_____ 9_____ 10_____

Transport

Match the words with the description:

Bike	It has 4 wheels and you drive it
Car	Place where the bus stops
Lorry	You get on with many people and pay money
Bus stop	Place where the train stops
Plane	It flies in the sky
Station	It has 2 wheels
Bus	A train which goes under the ground
Underground	You pay a man to drive you in this car
Taxi	It is very big and it carries many things

1) you/drive/can?

2) have/do/a/car/you?

3) like/do/you/flying?

4) you/can/bike/a/ride?

5) you/have/bike/a/do?

6) you/like/transport/do/what?

7) often/how/bus/a/take/you/do?

8) did/you/when/take/bus/last/a?

9) walking/do/you/like?

10) does/take/long/it/to/walk/school/how/to?

11) is/what/underground/nearest/station/your?

12) much/every/how/is/your/ticket/week?

Extension – Write at least 3 more questions to ask your partner:

Driving and Delivery – What do they do?

> He drives a private car ( ) He flies a plane ( )
> He drives a train ( )   He delivers letters to your house ( )
> He drives a bus ( ) He delivers documents on a motorbike ( )
> He teaches people how to drive ( ) He drives a taxi ( )

Match the jobs to what they do:

1) Train driver:
_____

2) Bus driver:
_____

3) Postman:
_____

4) Driving Instructor:
_____

5) Chauffeur:
_____

6) Taxi driver:
_____

7) Pilot:
_____

8) Courier:
_____

Parts of a Car

Put these words in the correct place on the picture:

wheel	boot	door	windscreen
lights		mirror	handle
seat		steering wheel	tyre

Now put the words in alphabetical order:

1_____ 2_____ 3_____ 4_____ 5_____

6_____ 7_____ 8_____ 9_____ 10_____

Parts of a Car

Ted the Taxi Driver

Ted is a taxi driver. He drives a taxi in London.

He starts at 2 o'clock in the afternoon. He starts his car and he drives to the office. His manager tells him to pick up passengers.

Ted drives to the passengers, picks them up and asks them where they want to go. He drives the passengers to their destination. The meter in the taxi displays the fare for the journey. He collects the fare and gives them a receipt.

He finishes work at 12am. After work he drives home. He likes his job.

1) What is his job?

2) Where does he drive?

3) What time does he start?

4) Where does he drive the passenger?

5) What does Ted give the passenger?

6) What time does he finish?

7) What does he do after work?

8) Does he like his job?

Extension – write at least 3 more questions about the text:

Role-play: Conversation with a Taxi Driver

*Who says what? First read the text. Then put "**D**" for the driver and "**P**" for the passenger. Next put the sentences in the right order.*

To Destination

__A) Where abouts in Putney? ( )

__B) Hello, taxi! ( )

__C) Which house number? ( )

__D) Okay, let's go! ( )

__E) Hello there, sir! ( )

__F) Paradise Road. ( )

__G) Please could you take me to Putney. ( )

__H) Number 27, please. ( )

At Destination

__A) Thanks very much. How much is the fare? ( )

__B) Okay, here we are at Paradise Road. ( )

__C) Here's your change! ( )

__D) That's £17, please. ( )

__E) Thank you but please keep the change. ( )

__F) Here you are! ( )

__G) Thanks for the tip. Goodbye! ( )

Now practise with your partner:

Dave the Driving Instructor

Dave is a driving instructor. He lives in Sale, Manchester and works in the Salford area.

Dave teaches people how to drive a car. He started teaching driving 20 years ago. It is a difficult job because he must be very patient. After his lessons his students take the DVLA driving test. The test is very hard. He works flexible hours. Sometimes he works four hours a day and sometimes he works 8 hours a day. He also works at weekends.

His job is very tiring but he likes it.

1) What is his occupation?

2) Where does he live?

3) Where does he work?

4) When did he start teaching driving?

5) What test do his students take?

6) Is the test easy?

7) Does he work flexible hours?

8) How many hours a day does he work?

Extension – Make at least 3 more questions about the text:

Transportation Questions

1) drive/you/can?

2) have/do/licence/a/driving/you?

3) ride/you/can/bicycle/a?

4) ride/can/you/motorbike/a?

5) how/take/you/do/a/train/often?

6) bus/often/how/you/take/a/do?

7) how/you/do/go/college/to?

8) you/go/how/interviews/job/can/to?

9) favourite/what/is/transport/your?

10) you/did/drive/country/your/in?

11) ride/bike/a/did/you/your/country/in?

12) work/how/go/did/country/your/in/you/to?

Extension – Write at least 5 more questions to ask your partner:

Job Advertisement

> **Wanted: Mini Cab Driver**
>
> Mini cab driver required for busy office in south London. Immediate start.
>
> Hours: 2pm-11pm. Hourly rate: £11. 25 days' paid holiday. Perks: free uniform and good pension.

Read the job advert and answer the questions:

1) What is the job title?

2) Where is the job location?

3) When does the job begin?

4) What time does the job start?

5) What time does the job finish?

6) What are the wages?

7) How long is the holiday?

8) What are the perks?

Unit 6: Employability

Job Vocabulary

	Paper with your information
	Place where you work
	Place where you get a job
	Money you get every day/week
	Money you get every month
	Boss
	The hours your work
	Paper with your wage/salary
	Things you have done before
	Job
	Extra things you get in a job
	Paper to say you will take the job

job centre   CV   manager   working hours

wages   salary   payslip   occupation

workplace   experience   benefits   contract

Extension - now put the words in alphabetical order:

1_____ 2_____ 3_____

4_____ 5_____ 6_____

7_____ 8_____ 9_____

10_____ 11_____ 12_____

Filling Out an Application Form

First Name (s): _____   Last Name: _____

Date of Birth: _____

Gender: (Circle)   Male   Female

Address:

_____

_____

_____

Postcode: _____

NI number: _____

Previous Positions:

```
┌─────────────────────────────────────────────────────────────────┐
│                                                                 │
│                                                                 │
│                                                                 │
└─────────────────────────────────────────────────────────────────┘
```

Education:

```
┌─────────────────────────────────────────────────────────────────┐
│                                                                 │
│                                                                 │
│                                                                 │
└─────────────────────────────────────────────────────────────────┘
```

References:

```
┌─────────────────────────────────────────────────────────────────┐
│                                                                 │
│                                                                 │
└─────────────────────────────────────────────────────────────────┘
```

Contact Details:

Home Phone: _____   Mobile Phone: _____

Email Address: _____

NAME

ADDRESS

TEL NUMBER

EMAIL

DOB:

Languages: English,

Skills:

EDUCATION

DATE   SCHOOL NAME, PLACE

                 SUBJECTS

EXPERIENCE

DATE   COMPANY, PLACE

                 JOB

HOBBIES: Reading and walking.

Role-play: Looking for a job

Put these sentences in order:

At Reception:

__ I'm looking for a job.

__ Hello. Can I speak to the manager, please?

__ Please wait while I get him.

__ Yes. What's it regarding?

With Manager:

__ Can you do a trial shift?

__ Hello, I'm the manager.

__ Do you have a CV?

__ Yes, I can. I can do a trial shift anytime.

__ Hi, my name is _____ and I'm looking for a job.

__ Thanks, we'll call you next week about your trial.

__ Yes, here is my CV.

__ Thanks for the CV. We have a position in the kitchen.

__ That position sounds great!

"Who says...?"

Match the jobs with what they say:

1) "I have a letter for you"   soldier

2) "I'm going to kill you!"   postman

3) "Stop talking and sit down!"   vet

4) "Your cat is very sick"   teacher

5) "Run! There's a fire!"   actor

6) "Do you want a wash and cut?"   fireman

7) "I grow many vegetables"   pilot

8) "Get out of your car and put your hands up"   artist

9) "We are flying at 35,000 feet"   landlord

10) "Are you sick?"   reporter

11) "I like to paint pictures"   barber

12) "It will be sunny today"   weatherman

13) "Your rent is late"   policeman

14) "Open your mouth and say "ahhhh!""   farmer

15) "I can't remember my words"   nurse

16) "What do you think of…?"   doctor

17) "Doctor, can I help you?"   waiter

18) "Your seat is number 34D next to the window"   secretary

19) "Do you want another glass of wine?"   stewardess

20) "I'm sorry, Mr Smith isn't here right now"   dentist

Jobs – questions

1) job/what/you/did/do?

2) you/which/did/area/in/work?

3) what/the/was/address/job/of/your?

4) there/long/did/work/you/how?

5) time/what/did/start/you?

6) what/did/time/you/finish?

7) did/you/your/like/job?

8) job/what/in/this/did/do/you/country?

9) of/was/what/the/your/name/boss?

10) job/was/your/good?

11) job/was/difficult/your?

12) what/you/job/want/do/do/to?

Extension – write at least 5 more questions to ask your partner:

Qualities – Danny the Doorman

Danny is a hard-working doorman at a bar in West London. He is a reliable worker. He works every night from 6pm to 2am. Danny is punctual – he is never late for work. He is also well-qualified – he studied how to be a doorman for 3 months at the local college, so he is very intelligent.

At the bar he is very polite to the customers – always saying "thank you" and "excuse me". He is very honest – if he finds money, he always gives it to his boss.

Danny works well with all the other staff at the bar. He is a team player. He likes his job.

Match the qualities with their meaning:

Hard-working	Always on time/never late
Reliable	Clever
Punctual	Works hard
Well-qualified	Has many certificates/diplomas
Intelligent	Always comes to work
Polite	Works well in a team
Honest	Uses kind words
Team-player	Always tells the truth

1) What is Danny's occupation?

2) Where does he work?

3) What are his working hours?

4) How long did he study to be a doorman?

5) What does he do if he finds money?

Occupations: what do they do?

1) She cuts hair: _____.

2) He brings you food in a restaurant: _____.

3) He cleans: _____.

4) She helps people in a shop: _____.

5) He serves beer in a pub: _____.

6) He cooks food in a restaurant: _____.

7) He builds houses: _____.

8) He makes things with wood: _____.

9) She looks after small children: _____.

10) He helps old people: _____.

11) He washes dishes: _____.

12) He drives people in a car for money: _____.

13) She works on the till at a supermarket: _____.

14) He helps people in a building site: _____.

15) He works in a factory: _____.

16) He works for no money: _____.

carpenter	waiter	hairdresser	**cleaner**	*cashier*
volunteer	chef	builder	**care worker**	
kitchen porter	**labourer**	taxi driver	barman	
child-minder	**shop assistant**	*factory worker*		

Job Interview Questions

1) you/tell/a/about/can/me/little/yourself?

2) experience/what/you/do/have/this/area/in?

3) leave/why/did/your/company/last/you?

4) what/ideal/position/is/your?

5) skills/what/key/are/your?

6) your/what/weak/are/points?

7) qualifications/what/have/you/do?

8) do/can/you/shiftwork?

9) punctual/person/are/you/a?

10) greatest/what/your/is/achievement?

11) reliable/person/are/you/a?

12) available/when/you/are/start/to?

13) questions/any/have/do/you?

Make 5 at least more questions to ask your partner:

Jobs Crossword

Across	Down
2. she dances for money	1. he takes you to the police station
3. he gives you letters	3. he flies planes
8. he drives a train	4. she sings songs
10. you pay him rent	5. he grows vegetables
14. he shoots people with a gun	6. he paints pictures
16. he brings you food in a restaurant	7. she cuts your hair
17. he teaches you English	9. he helps you when you are sick
18. she serves you in a restaurant	10. you pay her rent
	11. he cooks food in a restaurant
	12. he looks at your teeth
	13. he works in a church
	15. she helps the doctor

Unit 7: Health - Vocab

| first aid kit   plaster   bandage |
| tablet   ointment   syringe   scissors |
| safety pin   tweezers   sticky tape |

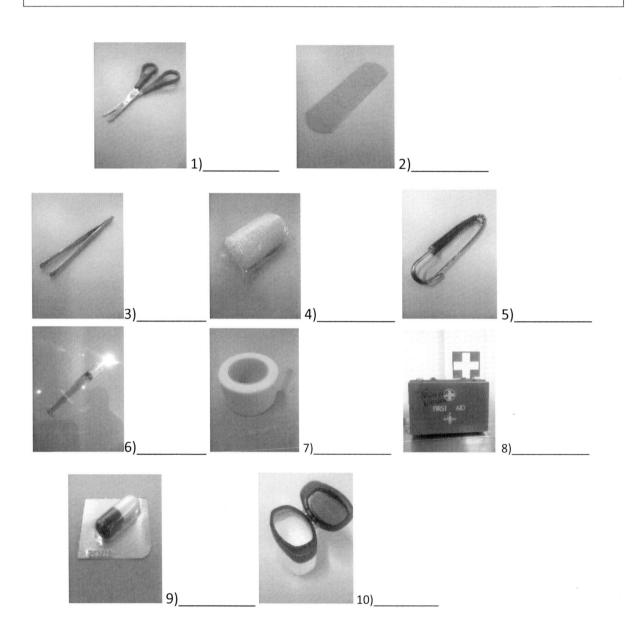

1)_____
2)_____
3)_____
4)_____
5)_____
6)_____
7)_____
8)_____
9)_____
10)_____

Now put the words in alphabetical order:

1_____ 2_____ 3_____ 4_____ 5_____

6_____ 7_____ 8_____ 9_____ 10_____

Health Vocab Match

Match the words with the meaning:

	he looks at your teeth
	it makes you better
	it drives you to hospital
	a place where you get medicine
	paper to get medicine
	he cuts you open
	a photo of inside your body
	red liquid in your body
	he helps you if you are sick
	she helps the doctor

dentist   nurse   doctor   ambulance   surgeon
medicine   chemist   prescription   blood   x-ray

Extension - now put the words in alphabetical order:

1_____ 2_____ 3_____ 4_____
5_____ 6_____ 7_____ 8_____
9_____ 10_____

Going to the GP

GP examines you	Call GP
Become sick	Make appointment with GP
Take medicine	Go home
Leave GP	Wait in the waiting room
Go to GP	Meet GP
GP writes a prescription	Go to chemist
Become better	Give prescription to chemist

Put the events in the right order:

1	2
3	4
5	6
7	8
9	10
11	12
13	14

Conversation at a GP

*Who says what? First, read the text. Then put "**GP**" for the <u>doctor</u> and "**P**" for the <u>patient</u>. Next, put the phrases in the correct order:*

__a) Goodbye. ___

__b) Hello, doctor. ___

__c) How long have you had it? ___

_1_ d) Hello, Mr Smith. ___

__e) Lie down and let me check you. ___

__f) What's the matter with you? ___

__g) I will give you a prescription for medicine. ___

__h) Well, I have a very bad stomach. ___

__i) I've had it for 3 days now. ___

__j) Take 3 a day for one week and come back next week. ___

__k) Okay, doctor. ___

__l) Thank you for checking, doctor. ___

__m) OK. I have finished checking, Mr Smith. ___

__n) Thank you, doctor. How many tablets should I take? ___

__o) Thank you, doctor. See you next week. ___

Now practise with your partner!

Health

Match the problems with the solutions:

Headache   drink hot lemon juice
Sore throat   drink water
Cough   put cold water on
Burn   rest
Fever   take aspirin
Backache   put cold water on head
Muscle ache   use a plaster
Cut finger   have a hot bath

1) you/do/exercise/do/much?

2) healthy/are/you/do/think/you?

3) last/when/you/did/see/doctor/a?

4) you/go/to/did/hospital/year/last?

5) feel/how/you/do/today?

6) healthy/do/you/eat/food?

7) much/doctor/how/a/is/country/in/your?

8) what/you/do/should/for/cold/a?

9) you/go/last/to/a/when/dentist/did?

10) you/had/have/operation/an/ever?

Extension – write at least 5 more questions to ask your partner:

Care Home – Literacy Check

kilburn car home is in kilburn on elgin avenue in london. there are thirty residents an ten staf.

every rooms hav a tolet and showar. The beds are big an ther is a phon in every rooms.

The residents eat Brekfast, Lanch and Diner. The foode is delicias. At nite they sumtimes hav a smal parti and they drinking a glas of wine or sometime they dinking coffe.

The residants playing games every days. They plays chess and kard Games. Its is a hapy car homes

Correct the mistakes in the text above and copy into the box below:

Questions

1) Where is the care home?

2) How many residents are there?

3) How many staff are there?

4) Are the beds big?

5) What do the residents eat?

6) Is the food delicious?

7) What do the residents sometimes drink?

8) How often do the residents play games?

9) What games do the residents play?

10) Is it a happy care home?

Extension – make at least 3 more questions about the text:

Care Questions

1) healthy/you/are?

2) you/tablets/do/take?

3) you/care/do/of/take/children?

4) your/old/are/how/parents?

5) did/a/you/when/plaster/use/last?

6) you/go/did/GP/to/last/the/year?

7) you/hospital/did/to/go/last/year?

8) injection/you/last/an/did/have/year?

9) a/you/be/do/to/carer/want?

10) you/to/do/be/want/childminder/a?

Extension – write at least 3 more questions to ask your partner:

Job Advertisement

Wanted: Child-minder

Child-minder needed in north London for 2 children (3 and 5 years old). Start next month.

Hours: 8am – 6pm. Daily rate: £70. 25 days' paid holiday. Perks: free meals.

Read the job advert and answer the questions:

1) What is the job?

2) Where is the job?

3) How old are the children?

4) When does the job begin?

5) What time does the job start?

6) What time does the job finish?

7) What are the wages?

8) What are the perks?

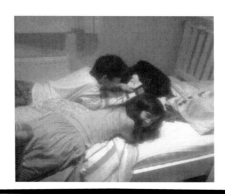

Unit 8: Money

Match the words with the meaning:

Bank	money you pay for your house/flat
Rent	place where you get money
Withdraw	paper money
Deposit	money of a country
Note	take money out of bank
Coin	put money in bank
Currency	round metal money

1) is/what/the/name/of/the/country/currency/in/your?

2) much/how/cost/does/rent/country/in/your?

3) how/much/cost/does/rent/London/in/your?

4) is/how/a/in/much/house/country/your?

5) your/is/country/expensive?

6) cheap/is/in/what/country/your?

7) you/spend/on/what/do/your/money?

8) every/much/you/how/do/spend/week?

9) much/how/money/have/do/you/pocket/in/your?

10) bank/is/the/what/name/of/your?

Extension – write at least 5 more questions to ask your partner:

Using a Cash Point – How to Withdraw Cash

Put these tasks in the right order:

Take money	Put bank card in
Select "withdraw cash"	Go to cash point
Take bank card out	Press "enter"
Type in PIN number	Select amount
Put money in wallet/purse	Take receipt

Write the tasks in order below:

1)	6)
2)	7)
3)	8)
4)	9)
5)	10)

Money: At the Bank

Yesterday John went to the bank. He opened the door and stood in the queue of people. The bank was very busy. There were 10 people in the queue.

At the counter he paid his gas bill. His bill was £110. He paid in notes and coins. When he finished he went to the cash point. He typed in his PIN number. Next, he checked his balance. He had £1,000 in his account. Then he withdrew £500 because he wanted to pay his rent. He put the money in his wallet and went home.

1) Where did John go yesterday?

2) How many people were in the queue?

3) What bill did he pay at the counter?

4) How much was his gas bill?

5) How much money did he have in his account?

6) How much did he withdraw?

7) Why did he want to withdraw money?

8) After his withdrawal, how much did he have left?

Extension – write at least 3 more questions about the text:

Opening a Bank Account – Conversation

*Who says what? First, read the conversation. Then put "**C**" for the <u>customer</u> and "**S**" for the <u>staff</u> at the bank. Next, put the phrases in the correct order:*

__I'd like to open a bank account, please. ( )

__Excuse me, please. ( )

__Certainly. A current account or a savings account? ( )

__What ID do I need? ( )

__Hello, sir. How can I help you? ( )

__OK, here is my ID. ( )

__That will do nicely, sir. Please take a seat. ( )

__A current account, please. ( )

__To open a current account, you need two forms of ID. ( )

__You need a passport and proof of address. ( )

Opening a Bank Account – Filling Out an Application Form

Fill out using BLOCK CAPITALS:

First Name (s): _____ Last Name: _____

Date of Birth: _____

Gender: (Circle)   Male   Female

Address:

_____

_____

_____

Postcode: _____

Time at Current Address: _____

NI number: _____

Marital Status: _____

Occupation: _____

Nationality: _____

Country of Birth: _____

Contact Details:

Home Phone: _____

Work Phone: _____

Mobile Phone: _____

Email Address: _____

Bill's Budget

Bill works 5 days a week as a barman at the local pub. He earns £400 a week before tax. When he gets his wages, his employer makes deductions for tax and national insurance. He pays £100 income tax and £40 national insurance. His take-home pay is £260 a week. He pays his landlord £150 a week rent. After this he makes a budget. He spends £60 a week on food and £30 a week on utilities (gas, water, electricity and phone). He spends the remaining £20 on entertainment - he likes to drink beer and play bingo at the weekend.

1) What is his occupation?

2) How much does he earn before tax?

3) What deductions does his employer make for tax?

4) What deductions does his employer make for national insurance?

5) What is his take-home pay?

6) How much does he spend on food?

7) How much does he spend on utilities?

8) What utilities does he spend money on?

9) How much does he spend on entertainment?

10) What entertainment does he like?

Extension – make at least 3 more questions about the text:

Unit 9: Maths: Shapes

Match the words with the shapes:

Square   Triangle   Rectangle   Cylinder   Circle   Cube   Cuboid   Sphere

Match the words to the symbols:

Plus   Subtract   Add   More than   Less than   Equals
Greater than   Multiply   Smaller than   The same as   Divided by
Times   Minus   Take away

+ _____, _____

- _____, _____, _____

× _____, _____

÷ _____,

> _____, _____

< _____, _____

= _____, _____

Self-check

Draw a square...					Draw a circle...

Draw a triangle...					Draw a rectangle...

Draw a cube...					Draw a cuboid...

Draw a sphere...					Draw a cylinder...

Write the sign for plus... _____

Write the sign for minus... _____

Write the sign for divide... _____

Write the sign for multiply... _____

Write the sign for greater than... _____

Write the sign for less than... _____

Questions

1) What is a sum?

2) What is a number pattern?

3) What is a right angle?

4) How many sides does a cube have?

5) How many edges does a triangle have?

Number Patterns

Complete these number patterns then write the number patterns:

1) 2   4   6   _   10   12   14   = e.g. It goes up by 2

2) 3   6   _   12   15   _   21   = _____

3) 10   _   30   40   _   _   70   = _____

4) _   8   _   16   _   24   28   = _____

5) 5   _   15   _   25   _   35   = _____

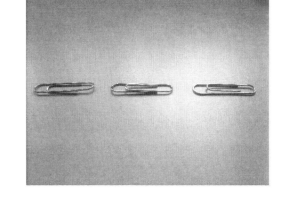

Most and Least

1) Eliza ordered 10 paperclips and Dahira ordered 5. Who ordered the least?

_____ ordered the least.

2) Sue sold 20 tickets and Roger sold 22. Who sold the least?

_____ sold the least.

3) Frank bought 3 litres of juice and Kim bought 2½ litres. Who bought the most?

_____ bought the most.

4) John has 10 books and Sarah has 5. Who has the most?

_____ has the most.

5) Kate slept 7 hours and Ralph slept 5. Who slept the least?

_____ slept the least.

Maths Questions

Put these questions in the correct order:

1) sides/many/does/triangle/have/a/how?

2) many/how/does/corners/square/have/a?

3) is/what/six/six/times?

4) circle/many/sides/does/have/a/how?

5) is/heavier/10kg/which/5kg/or?

6) everyday/what/is/object/sphere/a?

7) shape/usually/what/window/is/a?

8) is/four/by/two/divided/what?

9) is/what/25%/fraction/a/as?

10) tallest/in/room/who/the/the/is/person?

11) is/what/an/number/odd?

12) what/even/is/an/number?

Extension – write at least 5 more questions to ask your partner:

Unit 10: Citizenship – Vocab

1) _____ 2) _____ 3) _____

4) _____ 5) _____ 6) _____

7) _____ 8) _____ 9) _____ 10) _____

> double decker bus   policeman   Houses of Parliament
> Tower Bridge   St Paul's Cathedral   London Eye   black cab
> Trafalgar Square   Piccadilly Circus   Buckingham Palace

Now put the words in alphabetical order:

1_____ 2_____ 3_____ 4_____

5_____ 6_____ 7_____ 8_____

9_____ 10_____

The UK

Put these words in the spaces:

Edinburgh/Welsh/London/daffodil/people/Scottish/Cardiff/Belfast/1,500,000/Thames

There are 4 countries in the UK: England, Scotland, Wales and Northern Ireland. The flag is called the Union Jack.

England has 53,000,000 people. The capital city is London. About 9,000,000 people live in _____. The name of the big river in London is the _____. The flag of England is called the George Cross.

Scotland has 5,000,000 people. The capital city is _____. People from Scotland are called _____.

Wales has about 3,000,000 _____. The capital of Wales is called _____. The national flower of Wales is called the _____. People from Wales are called _____. Many Welsh people like rugby.

Northern Ireland has _____ people. The capital city is called _____.

The UK

1) do/live/you/where/UK/the/in?

2) like/you/in/living/UK/the/do?

3) like/house/you/your/do/UK/in/the?

4) favourite/in/place/what/your/is/London?

5) city/UK/the/what/favourite/in/your/is?

6) British/like/do/food/what/you?

7) like/you/weather/do/British?

8) did/job/what/you/in/do/Britain?

9) you/come/why/Britain/did/to?

10) best/what/in/your/is/UK/the/experience?

11) long/you/how/in/UK/the/have/lived?

12) been/ever/have/London/on/the/Eye/you?

Write at least 6 more questions about the UK to ask your partner:

13)

14)

15)

16)

17)

18)

Famous British People: Winston Churchill

Read the text and put these words in the spaces below:

1965/1874/politician/American/Oxford/Harrow School/1945/1965

Winston Churchill was a famous _____, army officer and writer. He was born in _____ and died in _____. He was born in Blenheim Palace near _____. His father was English and his mother was _____. When he was young, he studied at _____ in London, which is one of the best schools in the country.

He was Prime Minister twice. The first time he was Prime Minister was from 1940 to _____. In this time Britain was at war with Germany in World War Two. The second time was from 1951 to 1955. When he died in _____ there was a big funeral in London.

Copy the text below:

Review of the UK

1) Who is the queen of England?

2) Where does the queen of England live?

3) Who is the next king of England?

4) What are the 4 countries of the UK?

5) What are the capitals of the 4 countries in the UK?

6) How is the weather in the UK now?

7) What's the currency in Ireland?

8) How many people are there in London?

9) What is the name of the prime minister?

10) Who was the last prime minister?

11) Who was Diana?

12) Who is Prince William's wife?

13) What is Prince William's brother's name?

14) What is the name of the river in London?

15) What is the name of the big clock in London?

16) Name 4 big parks in London.

17) Name 4 museums in London.

18) Name 5 stops on the Central Line.

19) In what park can you find deer?

20) When was the Great Fire of London?

Unit 11: Festivals - vocab

1)_____ 2_____ 3)_____

4)_____ 5)_____ 6)_____

7)_____ 8)_____ 9)_____ 10)_____

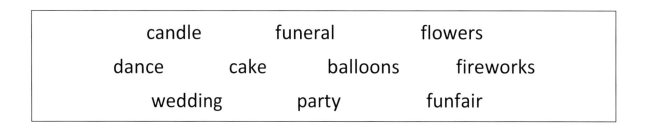

candle	funeral	flowers
dance	cake	balloons	fireworks
wedding	party	funfair

Now put the words in alphabetical order:

1_____ 2_____ 3_____ 4_____ 5_____

6_____ 7_____ 8_____ 9_____ 10_____

Festivals: Easter

Easter is very important for Christians. Easter is in March or April every year. On Good Friday people go to church. Jesus died on Good Friday. On Easter Sunday people go to church again. Many parents give chocolate eggs to their children. On Easter Sunday they have a big meal. People eat roast chicken, roast potatoes and carrots. They drink wine with the meal. After the meal they relax and watch TV.

1) When is Easter?

2) What do people do on Good Friday?

3) When did Jesus die?

4) Where do people go on Easter Sunday?

5) What do many people give to their children?

6) When do people have a big meal?

7) What do people eat?

8) What do they drink with the meal?

Extension – write at least 3 more questions about the text:

Festivals: A British Wedding

Most British weddings are in a church. Friends and family go to church for the wedding. The man wears a suit. The woman wears a white dress. After church they have a big wedding party. They invite many friends and relatives. They eat a lot of food. They drink beer or wine. They play music and people dance. Everyone is very happy.

After the party the man and woman go on holiday. The holiday is called a 'honeymoon.'

1) Where are most British weddings?

2) Who goes to the church?

3) What does the man wear?

4) What does the woman wear?

5) When do they have a big wedding party?

6) What do they eat?

7) What do they drink?

8) Where do the man and woman go after the party?

Extension – Write at least 3 more questions about the text:

A Wedding in My Country

Fill in the gaps about a wedding in your country:

Most weddings in _____ (my country) are in a _____. Friends and family go to the _____. The man wears a _____. The woman wears a _____. After, they have a big wedding party. They eat _____. They drink _____. They _____. Everyone is _____.

After the party the man and the woman _____.

Copy the text above into the box below:

Fred's Favourite Festival

My favourite festival in my country is Christmas. In December we decorate the Christmas tree with lights and candy. On December the 24th we celebrate Christmas Eve. We drink beer or wine and have a nice meal. This is the last day to do Christmas shopping.

On Christmas Day we wake up early and give each other presents. We open the presents and we eat breakfast. We eat Christmas dinner at 2 o'clock. We eat turkey, roast potatoes, carrots, Brussel sprouts and Yorkshire puddings. For dessert we have Christmas pudding or Christmas cake. We drink wine with the meal. After, we relax all day and watch TV. At 3 o'clock is the Queen's speech. After the speech we play games with the family. We don't eat dinner in the evening but we have light snacks for example, sausage rolls.

1) When is Christmas Eve?

2) When do people decorate the tree?

3) What do people drink on Christmas Eve?

4) When is the last day to do Christmas shopping?

5) What time do people eat Christmas dinner?

6) What do people drink with the meal?

7) What do people do after dinner?

8) What is on TV at 3pm?

Extension – Write at least 3 more questions about the text:

Festivals

Match the festivals with what you do:

Valentine's Day   decorate pumpkins
Easter   watch fireworks
Halloween   wrap presents
Guy Fawkes Night   drink beer and sing
Christmas Eve   eat turkey and give presents
Christmas Day   eat chocolate eggs and pray
New Year's Eve   buy chocolates and flowers

1) favourite/what/is/festival/your?

2) what/do/have/you/festivals/country/in/your?

3) birthday/when/your/is?

4) what/you/did/do/last/on/your/birthday?

5) mother's/do/day/celebrate/you?

6) celebrate/do/day/you/father's?

7) have/do/you/Valentine's/in/your/Day/country?

8) in/fireworks/your/when/country/do/watch/you?

9) in/your/what/country/do/do/you/at/weddings?

10) country/your/do/do/you/in/what/New/on/Year's/Eve?

Extension – Write at least 5 more questions to ask your partner:

My Country

David comes from England. He is 42 years old. He lives in Richmond. It is a big town near London. His nationality is British. He speaks English and a little French.

England has four seasons. In the winter it is cold and it rains a lot. In spring the flowers come out and it is a little warmer. In summer it is warm but not very hot. In summer many people go to the beach if it is a nice day. In autumn it is cool and the leaves fall from the trees.

1) Where does David live?

2) What is his nationality?

3) What languages does he speak?

4) How many seasons does England have?

5) When does it rain a lot?

6) When do the flowers come out?

7) Is it very hot in summer?

8) When do many people go to the beach?

9) When is it cool?

10) When do the leaves fall from the trees?

Extension – make at least 3 more questions about the text:

My Country

Put these words in order to make questions:

1) come/from/where/you/do?

2) in/country/where/you/did/your/live?

3) your/country/hot/is/summer/in?

4) many/how/have/do/you/seasons/country/your/in?

5) country/cold/winter/in/is/your?

6) nice/where/is/your/country/in?

7) food/what/eat/you/do/country/your/in?

8) like/you/do/your/country?

9) of/country/what/capital/is/the/your?

10) leader/who/is/of/the/country/your?

11) have/do/many/friends/country/in/you/your?

12) do/what/miss/you/country/your/in?

Extension – Write at least 5 more questions to ask your partner:

Unit 12: Describing
Describing People Vocab

Match the words to the meanings:

	nice to people
	has a lot of hair
	hair under the nose
	very fat
	hair around mouth
	high
	doesn't look nice
	nice-looking woman
	nice-looking man
	thin

| beard | overweight | hairy | moustache | friendly |
| slim | handsome | beautiful | tall | ugly |

Extension - now put the words in alphabetical order:

1_____ 2_____ 3_____ 4_____ 5_____

6_____ 7_____ 8_____ 9_____ 10_____

Describing People

Fill in the gaps with the correct word:

old/black/beard/brown/tall

He has _____ eyes and he has _____ hair. He has a long grey _____. He is 40 years _____. He is 1.8 metres _____.

glasses/tall/long/blonde/brown

She has _____ eyes and _____, _____ hair. She is 1.6 metres _____. She wears _____.

Now write about you:

Describing People and Things

| big   small   tall   short   fat   slim   handsome |
| ugly   dangerous   safe   lovely   friendly   hairy   unfriendly |
| crazy   interesting   tasty   disgusting   beautiful |

Put these words into the correct column:

Good	Bad	Good or bad

Talk about yourself and your things:

My house/flat is ……………………………………………………………………………………………

My country is ………………………………………………………………………………………………

London is ……………………………………………………………………………………………………

The UK is ……………………………………………………………………………………………………

My town is …………………………………………………………………………………………………

My friend is …………………………………………………………………………………………………

My mother/father is ……………………………………………………………………………………

My cousin is …………………………………………………………………………………………………

My brother/sister is ……………………………………………………………………………………

My neighbour is …………………………………………………………………………………………

My Family – Literacy Check

Correct the mistakes:

my name is david. I live in richmond near london. I have on Brother his name is tom. i hav to sisters. They are called erica and susan.

mye father is a docter. He works in a hospital. he like his job.

My mather is a cashier. She work in a shop in london. she work at weekends.

i lik me family!

Copy the correct version and write it below:

Family and Relationships

1) you/are/married?

2) have/you/do/brothers?

3) have/sisters/do/you?

4) many/how/brothers/sisters/and/have/do/you?

5) is/what/your/name/mother's?

6) father's/what/your/name/is?

7) family/does/live/where/your?

8) have/do/you/uncles/aunts/and?

9) have/cousins/you/do/many/how?

10) you/do/have/pet/a?

11) has/a/job/father/your/got?

12) in/family/your/who/like/do/you/best?

Now write at least 6 more questions:

My Friend – Literacy Check

Correct the mistakes:

my Best frend name is paul. His 40 yers old. he live in hampton near london. he work in a banke in London. he have on brother called fred.

We met at schol 20 yers ago.

we meet every weeks. We go to the pub and drinking beer together. We talking about footballs and work. Sometimes we going shoping together.

His hobby is footbal. he play every saturdays in the Park with he frinds. i lik me bist frind!

Copy the correct version and write it below:

Friends

1) best/friend's/name/is/your/what?

2) live/your/friend/where/best/does?

3) what/is/friend's/your/occupation/best?

4) old/how/best/is/friend/your?

5) meet/where/you/best/did/your/friend?

6) have/you/do/friends/many?

7) do/you/what/friends/with/do/your?

8) often/how/you/meet/do/friends/your?

9) old/how/your/are/friends?

10) see/you/when/did/friends/your/last?

11) talk/about/your/with/friends/what/you/do?

12) have/you/British/friends/do/any?

Extension - now write at least 3 more questions:

Manufactured by Amazon.ca
Acheson, AB